Heroes and Villains of the

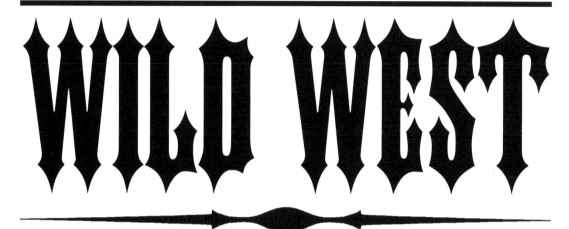

WILD WEST

Annie Oakley

by John Hamilton

ABDO & Daughters
PUBLISHING

Published by Abdo & Daughters, 4940 Viking Dr., Suite 622, Edina, MN 55435.

Cover Photo by: Buffalo Bill Historical Center
Inside Photos by:
Buffalo Bill Historical Center: pp. 5, 7, 9, 13, 14, 21, 22, 25, 27, 28
Bettmann: pp. 11, 16, 23, 24
Archive Photos: p. 19
John Hamilton: p. 17

Edited by Jill Wheeler

Library of Congress Cataloging–in–Publication Data
Hamilton, John, 1959–
    Annie Oakley / John Hamilton
      p. cm. — (Heroes & villains of the wild West)
    Includes bibliographical references (p. 31) and index.
    Summary: A biography of the markswoman and performer who achieved fame with Buffalo Bill Cody's Wild West Show.
    ISBN: 1-56239-563-7
1. Oakley, Annie, 1860-1926—Juvenile literature. 2. Shooters of firearms—United States—Biography—Juvenile literature. 3. Frontier and pioneer life—West (U.S.)—Juvenile literature. [1. Oakley, Annie, 1860-1926. 2. Entertainers. 3. Sharpshooters. 4. Women—Biography.]
I. Title. II. Series: Hamilton, John, 1959– Heroes & villains of the wild West.
GV1157.03H26 1996
796.3'092—dc20   95-45202
[B]   CIP
                                                            AC

Contents

The Peerless Lady Wing-Shot

On a bright August day in 1886, thousands of spectators flocked to Staten Island, New York, to watch Buffalo Bill Cody's Wild West and Congress of Rough Riders of the World. The Wild West was a Western-style circus. It was an amazing show featuring hundreds of authentic cowboys and Native Americans showing off their riding and roping skills and marksmanship. The Wild West had bucking broncos, the Pony Express, Indian raids, an attack on the Deadwood stagecoach, and a mock buffalo hunt.

At the center of this spectacle was the main attraction—Buffalo Bill himself. Decked out in buckskins, riding a magnificent steed with a Stetson hat on his head and a six-shooter in his hand, Cody was a living legend, a true Western hero. He rode around the giant ring, waving his hat to the standing-room-only crowd, which cheered wildly.

In another moment, though, Cody would be upstaged. The crowd shifted its full attention to a woman galloping into the ring sidesaddle, a Winchester rifle gripped in her hands. It was Annie Oakley, markswoman and performer. She was the sensation of America and Europe because of her amazing accuracy with a rifle. Oakley almost never missed her target. The crowd roared its approval, anxious for her performance to begin.

Annie was a small woman, just under five-feet tall and 100 pounds. She wore proper, ladylike clothes for the time—a fine embroidered jacket, knee-length pleated skirt, and pearl-buttoned leggings. To add a Western flair, she wore a cowboy hat with a gold star pinned to its turned-up brim.

Annie hopped down off the horse and hoisted her rifle to her shoulder. Her husband and assistant, Frank Butler, began operating a mechanical device called a trap, which tossed clay pigeons and small glass balls into

Annie Oakley in Buffalo Bill Cody's Wild West show, 1888.

the air. Annie's gun blazed away, smashing target after target. She switched to a shotgun, then pistols, one in each hand. (She was ambidextrous, meaning she could shoot just as well in either hand.) There weren't many people who could outshoot Annie Oakley, man or woman. Buffalo Bill called her "the Peerless Lady Wing-Shot." Chief Sitting Bull, her friend and fellow performer in the Wild West show, gave her the name, "Little Sure Shot."

Annie astounded the audience by laying her gun down, then throwing five glass balls into the air at once. She leaped for her rifle and plugged each ball before it fell. For another trick, she snuffed out a cigar held in her husband's lips. After that, from 30 paces away, she split a playing card held edgewise, hit coins tossed into the air, then plugged an apple sitting atop her dog's head.

By the time Annie was finished shooting, she'd hit 99 out of 100 glass balls and shattered many more clay pigeons. At the end of her act, Annie pranced around, blowing kisses to her adoring fans. Before she left the ring, she leapt in the air and gave a little jump kick, something she did at the end of every performance. The crowd went wild.

Annie Oakley is remembered as a crack shot who opened doors for women shooters. Before her time with Cody's Wild West, she was one of the most well-known professional game hunters in America. She made hunting and shooting an acceptable activity for women. At the same time, she kept up an image of wholesomeness and clean living. Unlike other women associated with the West, like Calamity Jane or Belle Starr, Annie Oakley always thought of herself as a "lady." She was a hard-working woman who overcame poverty and prejudice in her childhood to become a skilled markswoman and an enduring legend of the West.

Annie Oakley performing a trick shot with a mirror.

Rough Childhood

She was born Phoebe Ann Moses on August 13, 1860, daughter of a poor farm family in Darke County, Ohio. Her mother and father, Susan and Jacob, had a lot of mouths to feed. Annie had four older sisters, and later would come a younger sister and brother. Life was hard because the soil on the farm was not very good, but the family made do.

Then, when Annie was five, tragedy struck during the winter of 1865. Her father had gone to the nearby town of Greenville for supplies, but had not yet returned when a fierce blizzard covered the countryside. It was well after midnight when the family finally heard the horse pull up to the front of the little log cabin. They went outside and through the swirling snow found Jacob on his horse, nearly frozen stiff. He lasted a few months, then finally died of pneumonia early the next year. He left Susan a widow with seven children to raise.

The next year Annie's oldest sister, Mary Jane, died of tuberculosis. Susan had to sell the farm and a pet cow to pay for medical and funeral bills. The family moved to a smaller farm and tried to make do with what little they had.

Annie was only six years old, but she knew she had to do something to help the family. She began making clever traps made of cornstalks and string. By baiting the traps with grains of corn, she was able to catch small birds that she brought home for her mother to cook.

Although the traps worked well, Annie knew the family needed bigger game to keep from starving. Over her mother's protests, she took her father's old cap-and-ball Kentucky rifle off the fireplace mantle, filled it with black powder, and headed for the woods.

Annie was naturally a good shot, and soon she was bringing home fresh meat. After a year of practice, she could go out in the field sure that her family would have enough to eat that night. Usually she hunted quail, squirrel, rabbit, and grouse. Her aim grew so good that she could almost

Annie Oakley with one of her shotguns.

always hit the animals through the head, the way her father had taught her, so that the meat would be free of lead shot.

Even though Annie was helping bring food to the family, things were still very bad. Her mother earned only $1.25 per week as a health nurse. Her many children were such a burden that she was forced to send some of them away to neighbors and friends who volunteered to help. When Annie was about nine years old, she was sent to live with a family that ran a local infirmary, where poor orphans and mentally ill people lived. While there, she learned to knit and sew. She earned money sewing for the inmates of the infirmary.

Soon she got an offer to live with another family. She was supposed to help a farm wife take care of their young baby. She thought she would be well paid and sent to school. Annie took the job, but soon found out she'd made a terrible mistake. The husband and wife abused Annie. They made her get up at four in the morning to milk the cows, then do dishes and feed the farm animals, weed the garden, and all sorts of other chores. Plus, she had to take care of the baby. She hated the husband and wife, calling them the "he-wolf" and the "she-wolf."

But Annie was a prisoner. Her new employers wouldn't let her go. They kept her out of school and fed her poorly. Once Annie fell asleep while sewing. The wife hit Annie, then threw her out into the snow, where she nearly froze to death.

Annie finally ran away after nearly two years with the "wolves." She made her way home to the family farm. In the years that Annie had been gone, her mother had married a second time. Sadly, her new husband had died, leaving Susan with a baby girl to care for in addition to the rest of the family. Now Susan was married a third time, to a man named Joseph Shaw. But he was poor and not in good health, and Susan was sick with typhoid. Annie decided to earn her keep and help the family by going back to the infirmary to live and earn what little money she could.

During these years Annie finally learned to read and write. She also practiced sewing, which she learned to do well. But she missed the family farm, and the fresh air, and the wonderful feeling she got out in the woods while shooting for dinner. So Annie made up her mind to move back to the farm to be with her family.

This time the young Moses girl earned her keep by hunting. She was such a good shot by now that not only did she get enough meat for the family, she had enough left over to sell to a shop in town. Her game was in demand because she always shot the animals through the head, so people knew the meat would have no lead shot in it.

Shooting came naturally to Annie. In her autobiography, she wrote, "I don't know how I acquired the skill, but I suppose I was born with it." Her talent with a rifle helped save the family farm. With the money she earned selling extra meat, she was able to pay off the mortgage. Annie would never be poor again.

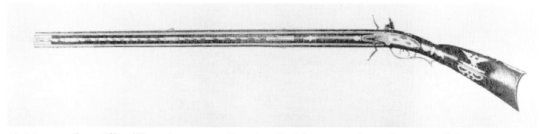

A Kentucky rifle like the one Annie Oakley used to hunt wild game.

Frank Butler

By the time she was a teenager, young Annie had become so good with her rifle that her sister Lydia urged her to compete in a shooting match. Annie agreed, and on Thanksgiving Day, 1875, she arrived at a field near the outskirts of Cincinnati, Ohio, ready to compete, even though she'd never shot at targets thrown from a mechanical trap before.

Her competition that day was a man by the name of Frank Butler. He was a championship shooter who toured the country giving exhibitions. Wherever he played he offered to shoot against any local marksman who wanted to take him on. Butler was a friendly man who neither smoked, drank liquor, nor gambled.

When Butler arrived at the site of the match that Thanksgiving Day, he was very surprised to see a young girl in a calf-length skirt, gun in hand, ready to compete against him. He laughed. Was *this* his competition for the day? Soon though, Annie would wipe the smile right off his face.

Butler shot first. He called out "pull," and a clay pigeon was sent flying into the air. He raised his gun to his shoulder, took aim, and fired. The pigeon exploded into a thousand tiny pieces of dust. "Dead bird!" came the call from the referee.

Now it was Annie's turn. "Pull!" she cried. The clay pigeon sailed out, but in an instant it too exploded, hit by Annie's gun. "Dead!" came the call.

Annie and Frank fired shot after shot, never missing until the 25th and last round, when Frank finally missed. Annie took her station, full of confidence and ready to shoot. "Pull!" she yelled. In her autobiography she wrote, "I stopped for an instant before I lined my gun. . . I knew I would win!" Sure enough, her shot smashed the pigeon, winning her the match.

Annie took home $25 for that day's work, the first of thousands of matches she would win in her lifetime. Frank Butler wasn't too upset about losing to such a sweet young girl. He was very impressed with

Frank Butler, left, holding shotgun, competes at a skeet range.

Annie's shooting ability. Butler wanted to see her again, so he gave Annie and her family passes to his shooting exhibition.

Although Butler put on a good show, Annie was more interested in his pet poodle, George. Butler did one trick where he shot an apple off the dog's head. George picked up a piece of the apple and brought it over to Annie, who was sitting close by. After the match, she sent the poodle her thanks for the exhibition. "George" responded by sending candy. So began the romance between Annie and Butler. Even though he was 10 years older than she, Annie liked Frank's good humor and father-like attitudes. Because she spent most of her childhood without a father, he represented a sense of security to her. Plus, they had a lot in common. They shared the same love of shooting, and Frank also grew up poor, finding success through hard work and determination. Frank adored Annie, and finally asked her to be his wife. In 1876, a year after they first competed against each other, Annie and Frank were married.

The Wild West of Annie Oakley

Ohio

Darke County
•Greenville

•Cincinnati

On the Road

Annie spent the next several years helping Frank with his shooting shows. They traveled all over the country, working in circuses and vaudeville theaters. It was quite a change for the poor country girl who had never before been more than a few miles from home. Annie enjoyed traveling and seeing the big cities in which they worked.

One day Frank's shooting partner got sick before a show, and Annie volunteered to help set up targets. But during the performance, she rebelled and insisted on shooting every other trick. The crowd went wild over this tiny woman who could shoot with such amazing ability, and Frank soon had her join him permanently in his act.

It was during this time that Annie began using the stage name Annie Oakley. She never really liked the name Moses, and wanted something that sounded better when she entered the shooting ring. No one really knows why she picked Oakley. Maybe it was just because it had such a strong ring to it. In any case, the crowds adored her. To win them over, she would often miss the first shot on purpose, pout and stamp her foot. But then she hit every target afterwards. Her skill with a gun was amazing. Annie Oakley soon became a well-known name among shooters and sporting enthusiasts.

Annie was very careful to save her money. Her early years of poverty and hardship had taught her how important it was to be frugal and to work hard for an honest living. She sewed her own costumes, something she would do for the rest of her stage career. She also never forgot her mother back in Ohio. Annie usually sent home part of her paycheck when she was on the road, and between shows she and Frank visited Susan often.

During these years Annie took up the cause of encouraging women to learn the sport of shooting. She even started giving lessons to women interested in learning from her. Before this time, shooting was thought of as a "man's" sport. But Annie knew from experience that a woman could be just as fine a shooter as any man. She wanted women to know how good it felt to get out in the field and hunt, or even just shoot clay pigeons for sport. She also thought it was important for women to know how to properly handle a gun in case they had to defend themselves or their households.

Annie Oakley, right, teaches a student to shoot at flying targets.

The Wild West

In 1885, Annie and Frank auditioned for Buffalo Bill Cody's Wild West show. The pair had been playing the circus and vaudeville circuit for a few years now, and felt they needed a step up in their careers. The Wild West was just what they were seeking.

At first, Cody wasn't sure such a small woman could handle the kinds of big guns that would be required, but Annie knew she could shoot anything they put in her hands. Cody agreed to see their act in Louisville, Kentucky, when the Wild West played there in the spring.

Annie and Frank spent a few weeks practicing at gun clubs for the big day, then took a train to Louisville. When they arrived at the field where the Wild West was to play, nobody was there to greet them. They thought they were early, so Annie set up some targets and started practicing.

After performing some of her more difficult tricks, and shattering every target, an elderly man with a derby hat and a cane came out from a corner of the grandstand. He had been watching her practice from there. According to Annie, the man ran toward them and said, "Fine! Wonderful! Have you got some photographs with your gun?" The man turned out to be Nate Salsbury, Buffalo Bill's partner in the Wild West. He hired Annie and Frank on the spot.

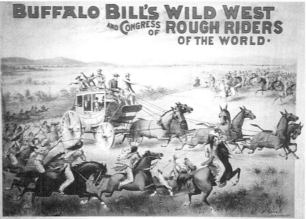

A publicity poster announcing Cody's Wild West show.

Their first year with the Wild West was a hard one. They had to get used to a very busy schedule, which had them traveling thousands of miles by train all over the East Coast and up into Canada. But Annie soon got used to this new life. She was happy to be steadily employed, and she liked how organized the Wild West was. She practiced her shooting skills every day and drew in her share of fans among the crowd.

When Annie skipped into the arena, waving her rifle over her head and smiling to the crowd, the applause grew thunderous. She had begun pinning medals she'd won at shooting matches to the front of her blouse, and these jingled as she waved to the crowd. Spectators were amazed at her shooting abilities. She added new tricks to her routine, including snuffing out candles with a rifle and shooting glass balls thrown into the air while riding horseback. And then, when her act was over, she blew kisses to her fans and did her trademark jump kick as she skipped out of the arena.

The crowds loved her so much that Buffalo Bill soon gave her top billing as "Miss Annie Oakley, the Peerless Lady Wing-Shot." By now Annie's husband, Frank Butler, knew that the spotlight was on his wife. He stepped aside and acted as Annie's manager and helper during her act. Although he was a great shot, and in later years would continue to put on exhibitions and shoot for sport, he would never achieve the fame that his wife earned for herself.

When the Wild West rolled into town, Annie and Frank had a tent pitched just for them right on the stadium grounds, alongside tents for Buffalo Bill and Nate Salsbury. Annie preferred sleeping in the big tent instead of a hotel room. The tent was furnished with chairs, rugs, and curtains to give them a nice home-away-from-home feeling.

After shows, Annie often had children come to her tent to visit. She was famous for being kind and generous to children, especially orphans. This wasn't surprising considering her hard childhood. She understood how important it was to be kind to children, especially those who were poor or who didn't have parents to love them.

William "Buffalo Bill" Cody.

Little Sure Shot

Annie also was kind to the many Native Americans who toured with the Wild West. They often came to her with problems they had, knowing she would be understanding. In a time when there was much prejudice toward Indians, Annie often spoke up about how poorly Native Americans were treated, and about the many injustices and terrible living conditions on the reservations.

The famous Sioux Chief Sitting Bull became good friends with Annie during their time together touring with the Wild West. Annie actually had met Sitting Bull in 1884 in Minneapolis, Minnesota. The old chief had received permission to leave Standing Rock Indian Reservation, in the Dakota Territories, in order to tour big "white men" cities. While in Minneapolis, he attended a Western show in which Annie and Frank were performing. Sitting Bull was bored with the show, but when Annie skipped onto the stage, guns blazing, he perked right up. He met her later after the show.

Annie thought Sitting Bull was a nice old gentleman. The Sioux chief thought Annie was so wonderful that he insisted on adopting her to replace one of his daughters who was killed at the Battle of the Little Big Horn. He called Annie "Watanya Cecilla," or "Little Sure Shot."

Frank Butler, and then later Buffalo Bill, advertised Annie's relationship with Sitting Bull to draw in bigger crowds. They started calling Annie "the girl of the Western Plains." This name, and "Little Sure Shot," soon caught on among newspaper writers. Even though she was born in Ohio, Annie became associated with the American West. Strong-willed and straight-laced, confident of her abilities, a crack shot and expert horse rider, she represented the ideal Western character. Sitting Bull was proud to have her as an adopted daughter. Annie was equally fond of Sitting Bull, and considered him a faithful old friend.

In 1890, Sitting Bull was back at Standing Rock Reservation. Indian police tried to arrest him for stirring up trouble among his people. A

Chief Sitting Bull, who named Annie Oakley, "Little Sure Shot."

gunfight erupted, and when the shooting was over, Sitting Bull was dead, along with seven of his followers and six policemen.

Annie was broken-hearted over the loss of her friend. She was also angry at the conditions on the reservation that led to the shooting, and that things were so unfair for Native Americans. "Had he been a white man," she wrote, "someone would have been hung for his murder."

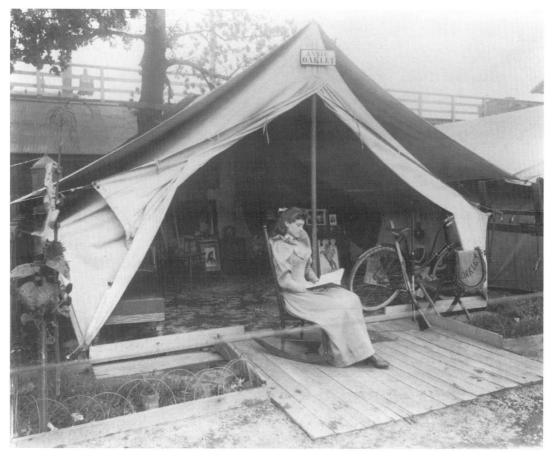

Annie Oakley reading in her tent at the Chicago World Fair in 1893.

Across the Atlantic

In 1887, Queen Victoria of England staged her Golden Jubilee, the 50th anniversary of her coronation. The Wild West show boarded a ship and set sail across the Atlantic Ocean, ready to join in the celebration.

During the voyage, their ship got caught in a bad storm. The Native Americans, who were already uneasy about traveling across the "big water," were sure they were going to die. Many of the other performers were ready to meet their maker as well. Annie stayed calm through the ordeal, even when the storm smashed the ship's rudder, setting them adrift for two days. Eventually, the captain regained control of his ship, and they were back on their way to England.

Queen Victoria

At that time in Europe, there was a lot of interest in the American West, and Buffalo Bill felt sure his overseas tour would be wildly successful. He wouldn't be disappointed. Situated in a field just outside London, the show drew half a million visitors during its first three weeks.

Annie quickly charmed the English audiences with her shooting and riding skills. Within a month the newspaper headlines were all praising this "shootist" from the American West who used her rifle with such unusual accuracy.

In June, Queen Victoria herself left Buckingham Palace and attended a special performance of the Wild West. After the show, the queen called Annie over to her velvet-draped viewing box. She told Annie, "You are a very clever little girl."

Leaves the Wild West

Annie and Frank stayed with the Wild West show for nearly 17 years, touring all over the United States and Europe. Because she grew up as a poor farm girl who rarely traveled more than a few miles from home,

Prince William

Annie was now happy to be seeing the world and rubbing elbows with famous people. Once, while giving a shooting exhibition in Berlin, Germany, she met Crown Prince William (who would later be called Emperor William II). He was very taken with Annie, and demanded to take part in her act. She obliged him by shooting the end off a lit cigarette while the prince held it in his lips.

Still, after so many years on the road, the hectic routine of the Wild West began to take its toll on Annie and Frank. Show business used to be fun for Annie, but as the years wore on it became more work and drudgery.

In 1901, Annie injured her spine after a train carrying the Wild West performers wrecked outside of Charlotte, North Carolina. Annie resigned from the Wild West so that she could take time to recuperate.

Nearly a year later, Annie began shooting again in matches and exhibitions. Then, in 1911, she joined another Western production, Vernon Seavers' Young Buffalo Show. Just as she had done in Cody's Wild West, Annie performed trick shots, rode horses, and delighted audiences with her girlish charm.

Annie Oakley on horseback in 1920. Note her signature at the bottom of the photo.

Retirement

In 1913, Annie Oakley finally retired, making her last appearance in Marion, Illinois. She and Frank were getting too old for the rigorous life of show business. By now she was in her mid-fifties, and Frank was well into his sixties. They decided to use the money they'd earned over the years and relax for a change.

They moved from place to place over the next decade, living in such places as the Carolinas and Florida. Even in retirement, Annie stayed active. She competed in numerous exhibitions and matches, and during World War I even taught young soldiers how to shoot. She also helped raise money for the Red Cross. A car accident in 1922 put her permanently in a steel leg brace, but she recovered enough to continue with her love of shooting.

In 1926, Annie moved back to Greenville, Ohio, to be close to her family. She was in poor health, but still kept up the bright optimism that many would remember her for. After a long illness, on November 3, 1926, Annie Oakley died peacefully in her sleep.

Broken-hearted over the loss of his beloved Annie, Frank Butler grew ill. Less than three weeks later, at the age of 76, Frank joined Annie in death. Today they are buried side by side in a cemetery near Greenville. The inscription on each tombstone simply says, "At Rest."

Annie Oakley teaching a young girl to shoot a rifle in 1920.

Annie Oakley sometime in the mid-1880s with one of her dogs.

Glossary

clay pigeon

A clay disk that is thrown as a flying target for skeet and trapshooting. It is also called a "bird."

Cody, Buffalo Bill (1846-1917)

A frontier buffalo hunter, U.S. Army scout and Indian tracker, Cody symbolized the American West through real-life feats and later through fiction and drama with his famous Wild West show.

Dakota Territories

A region established in 1861 that included present-day North and South Dakota, Wyoming, Montana, and a part of eastern Idaho.

Queen Victoria (1819–1901)

Queen of the United Kingdom of Great Britain and Ireland from 1837 to 1901. Also Empress of India from 1876 to 1901. She was very popular among her subjects. Her Golden Jubilee in 1887 was the cause of much public celebrating. Her reign of 63 years was the longest in the history of England, and is known as the Victorian age.

reservation

A section of land set aside by the United States government for use by an American Indian tribe or people.

shotgun

A shoulder-held firearm that shoots steel or lead pellets through a smooth bore. Commonly used in hunting birds.

sidesaddle

A common way for women to sit on a horse at the turn of the century. The saddle was designed so that the woman could sit with both legs on one side of the horse.

Sioux

A group of Native American people who lived on the Great Plains in what is now the Dakotas, Minnesota and Nebraska.

tuberculosis

A contagious disease that usually causes lesions, or sores, in the lungs of humans. Antibiotics have made tuberculosis much less common than it was at the turn of the century.

William II (1859-1941)

Emperor of Germany and king of Prussia from 1888-1918. Also known as Kaiser Wilhelm. His full name was Friedrich Wilhelm Viktor Albert. His policies helped start World War I. After Germany lost the war, he gave up the throne.

Winchester

A popular type of rifle. Annie Oakley often used a Winchester in her act, as well as guns made by Remington and Parker Brothers. She never played favorites by endorsing any particular gun. As she wrote, "The best gun is the gun that best fits the shooter."

Bibliography

Conlan, Roberta, Editor. (1993). *The Wild West*. New York: Time-Life Books.

Encyclopaedia Britannica, Volume VII, p. 456.

Havighurst, Walter. (1954). *Annie Oakley of the Wild West*. University of Nebraska Press, Lincoln, Nebraska.

Riley, Glenda. (1994). *The Life and Legacy of Annie Oakley*. University of Oklahoma Press: Norman and London.

Wilson, Ellen. (1962). *Annie Oakley, Young Markswoman*. New York: Macmillan Publishing Company.

Index